ACCEPT YOUR OWN AND BE FREE FROM MENTAL SLAVERY

BY

SHEIK CHARLES BROWN-EL

© 2003 by Sheik Charles Brown-EL.
All rights reserved.

No part of this book may be reproduced, stored in a retrieval system, or transmitted by any means, electronic, mechanical, photocopying, recording, or otherwise, without written permission from the author.

ISBN: 1-4107-6318-8 (e-book)
ISBN: 1-4107-6319-6 (Paperback)

Library of Congress Control Number: 2003093890

This book is printed on acid free paper.

Printed in the United States of America
Bloomington, IN

1stBooks - rev. 06/02/03

PROPHET NOBLE DREW ALI

PROPHET AND FOUNDER OF THE MOORISH

SCIENCE TEMPLE OF AMERICA

I would like to dedicate this brief manifestation of my thoughts to the last Prophet in these days, Noble Drew Ali, and the Moorish Science Temple of America, for it is through these sources that I continue to strive for greatness. It is the Prophet's words that I speak and have spoken, not my own, so I give him my highest honor for walking the path ahead of me that I can just walk inside his footprints that were left clearly cut. Also to my wife, Deputy Sheikess Trinae Brown-EL, my thanks for sharing the good times and thanks for being my friend.

TABLE OF CONTENTS

- AUTHOR'S FOREWORD ix

ACKNOWLEDGEMENTS xi

- INTRODUCTION xv
- CHAPTER 1: UPLIFT THE ASIATIC WOMAN . 2
- CHAPTER 2: MEN NEED A PATTERN FOR THEIR LIVES 10
- CHAPTER 3: NATION- BUILDING TIME 18
- CHAPTER 4: DIVINE AND NATIONAL ENLIGHTENMENT 26
- CHAPTER 5: MOORISH FLAG 32
- CHAPTER 6: WHY ARE WE MOORISH AMERICANS? 38

- CHAPTER 7: THE CHILDREN ARE OUR FUTURE 46
- CHAPTER 8: THOUGHT IS THE CAUSE OF IT ALL 52
- CHAPTER 9: ESTABLISH PRINCIPLES OF ACTION 60
- CHAPTER 10: ISLAMISM! 68
- CHAPTER 11: TURBAN AND FEZ 74
- CHAPTER 12: THE RISE TO GREATNESS 78
- REFERENCES 83
- MOORISH SCIENCE TEMPLE OF AMERICA, INC. CONTACT LIST 85

AUTHOR'S FOREWORD

Truth is one; your doubt is of your own raising. In this book is the truth to the best of my knowledge. It is in brief the blueprint to raise the Asiatic nation back to greatness.

If anyone has any disagreements, they can contact the author. Keep in mind that just because you don't believe a thing doesn't make it untrue; it just makes you an unbeliever.

Remember, according to all true and divine records there are no such terms as Negro, Black, or Colored attached to the human family. Peace, and may Allah the God of love bless our undertakings and us all.

Sheik Charles Brown-EL

ACKNOWLEDGEMENTS

I raise my thoughts above everything carnal to give praises to Allah. I give honor to the last Prophet in these days and times, Prophet Noble Drew Ali. I want to give honor to all who made my thought of writing possible either directly or indirectly. First, thanks goes to my brother and best friend, Sheik Joseph Young-BEY. Brother, I recognize that we are likened unto Moses and Aaron, and we still have much work to do for the uplifting of fallen humanity.

I give great honor to Timothy Dingle-EL-Noble Drew Ali in this era of time who is honored as Chief, Shiloh, and Judah by divine right and conquest.

To my teacher, leader, guide and father, National Grand Sheik Clarence Prather-EL, the master word for me has been and is "PLAN." His vision has been my vision for some time, because I have been molded and shaped in his image and likeness.

My family for whom I give praises to Allah. My beautiful wife, Queen Trinae Brown-EL, who is at the time of this writing pregnant with our second child, and my strong-willed daughter, Princess Naasira Brown-EL. Through them I truly have learned the meaning of Act 7 of the Divine Constitution and by-laws of the Moorish Science Temple of America. I also give high honor to my mother, Sister Donna M. Tolbert, as well as my grandparents, for putting up with me during the years of my trials when I was trying to find myself.

I give honor to my teacher Sheik Ronald Thorne-EL for instructing me. To Sheikess Betty Prather-EL and

Queen Beatrice Thorne-EL, for they have been good Moorish mothers to me. To Sheikess Yvonne Green-EL who gives me inspiration through words. To my sister Sheikess Yolanda Young-BEY, who has and continues to take good care of me in love, truth, peace, freedom and justice, and to my goddaughter and niece, Princess Asia Young-BEY. I love you, Moors; keep doing the will of Allah. I would also like to thank Sheikess Tiffany Jones-BEY, the Moorish attorney, whom I am grateful to have as my sister and friend.

I would like to give honor to Sheik Robin Carroll-EL for having the inspiration to draw the divine cover for this book. Keep being inspired to draw, big brother. I also would like to thank Chuck Herron and Suzanne Flinn from 1st Books library for all of their diligent and earnest assistance with getting this book published and ready to be distributed.

Last but definitely not least, to my grandmother Dorothy Mae Brown, who passed away due to heart problems before I even began working on this book. She has always inspired me. No matter what I have done or experienced, she always saw the best in me and labeled me her miracle baby. So she knew that Allah had his hands on me and would bless me to be a great person.

Sheik Charles Brown-EL

INTRODUCTION

In these times that we live in, everyone has customs and traditions that they live by as a nation, except the so-called Negro in America. We have been taught to be and exist a certain way that is far from the way our forefathers lived. It is imperative that we begin to love and accept ourselves the way that other nationalities do. When members of other nationalities meet, they hug and kiss as if they have known one another for years. *Latinos* are a great example of this type of love and race pride. Why do we as a people hate one another so much? If one of our sisters sees another sister that is not as fortunate as she is, instead of assisting her sister in adversity, she scorns and talks about her. These are some of the greatest problems that we need to look into with an aim to correct.

The mental condition of our people dates back to 1774, when the Moors were forced to serve other gods and other ideals of men. In the same year, the Moors were given the names of Negro, Black and Colored by the European nations. At that time, America had not gained its independence from Great Britain, so we had five years to answer to our name as Moors. Because we didn't, in the year 1779 the Moors disappeared off the face of the earth, according to documentation, and up come the names Negro, Black and Colored.

We were taught in school about General George Washington cutting down the proverbial cherry tree; the significance of the tree was the Moorish nation. The General was stating in signs and symbols that he had cut down a nation of people from their divine and national principles. The cherry tree is symbolic of the Moorish flag, which is a red flag with a five-pointed green star in the center. In taking away the flag of a nation, you take away the nation's identity. This is exactly how we lost our identity and began believing that we were Negroes, Blacks and Colored people. By clinging to these names, the furthest we can go back to trace ourselves through history is to slavery, because the Negro did not exist before 1774.

There are only two races on the earth, and those are Asiatic and European, though there are many nationalities. The Asiatic race was the first race on the earth, with Adam and Eve being the father and mother of the human family. Once they were cast out of the Garden of Eden they went into Asia, making their descendants Asiatics. Because of disobedience, some of their children were sent to the caves and hills of Europe where they lost their hue, and their descendants are European. European society has determined that there are five races. This was done to make you feel inferior to the so-called white race, because it separated the Asiatic race by our origins in the world. For example, the Indians they call red men, the Moors they call black men, and the whole continent of Europe they call white men; this makes it appear as if the European is dominant over all of the Asiatic race. This trickery came into existence through a German philosopher in the 1700s by the name of Johann F. Blumenbach. A man's nationality is based upon the geographical land that his forefathers' inhabited, and the so-called Negroes' nationality is Moorish

American not African American, because Africa is a continent that has at this time over 55 countries in it, and it is impossible to claim the whole continent.

During the time of slavery, the northwestern and southwestern shores of Africa were the lands that the Moors were taken from. This portion of land at that time was the old Moroccan empire. All of the Africans and their descendants are Moors, because they are descendants of Moroccans and born in America. We are not descendants of the present day Moroccans, as they are French, since the French invaded the land and amalgamated it. This is why if you meet someone from Morocco he or she will most likely have pale skin and appear to be of European descent. We, the so-called Blacks, whose true race is Asiatic, are descendants from the ancient Moabites who inhabited the northwestern and southwestern shores of Africa.

Prophet Noble Drew Ali founded the Moorish movement known as the Moorish Science Temple of America in 1913 A.D., to teach the Asiatics of America the truth about themselves and bring them back into the constitutional fold as Moorish Americans, so that they might be respected by the government under which we live and in the nations of the earth. To be a nation, you must proclaim your nationality and go back to the state of mind of your forefathers and begin to think as a nation.

Herein lies information and insight to get back into God's grace. A nation cannot stand divided; a nation cannot exist if it hasn't learned how to love, love first oneself and then love the world.

The people who oftentimes refer to themselves as black people are in a worse condition now than they were 200 years ago. Today, we are piled up in communities called ghettos, and the living conditions are terrible. The sisters are having child after child by different brothers who do not desire to be fathers. Our children are raised with the wrong message because they aren't taught love, truth, peace, freedom, and justice, which are the five highest principles known to man. They aren't taught the knowledge of themselves because nine times out of ten their parents have no knowledge of self and aren't seeking it. Because of these issues, we are tearing ourselves down. I pray that in this book will be light that will light up the minds of those who read it to make a drastic change in their condition if it is described, and to change the stereotype of the Asiatic race.

If I make any errors in my writing, they are on me. I am being guided and inspired by the great God-Allah to break down the barriers and plagues of my people in North America.

Also, in this book the so-called black people will be referred to as Asiatic, because this is the true race of our people. I love my race, and I desire to see us unify as a nation (Moorish American nation).

CHAPTER 1

UPLIFT THE ASIATIC WOMAN

*ACCEPT YOUR OWN AND BE FREE
FROM MENTAL SLAVERY*

The first step in building a nation and returning to our forefathers' way of thinking is to treat our women with reverence and love. Remember that there is only one way that a man can be produced, and that is through a woman. She is the closest creature to God-Allah, for in her womb she bears the nation.

The men in the Asiatic nation have got to discontinue viewing our women as sex symbols and displaying them on television and in music videos in the manner that we do. Woman is not made to gratify our loose desires and be a slave to man's passion, but to assist him in the toils of life. The blatant disrespect and disregard for the Asiatic woman is the greatest reason why the Asiatic nation is in the condition that it is in. We must teach our women that they are Queens and that they have an illustrious history, because the woman/mother is a child's first teacher and whatever she knows or feels she will instill into her baby, which in turn grows and matures as a product of its mother and begins to take on the attributes of the mother. If the mother doesn't know her worth and what she means to the building of the nation, then she can't teach it to her children. Our sisters must learn to respect themselves likewise in order for anyone else to respect them. Sisters, you must demand to be treated as the Queens that you are.

The European has affected us so deeply during the time of slavery with his customs and traditions that we now believe that only the right thing to do is to coexist with them as they live. But we have our own customs and traditions. The Asiatic woman should stop dressing so provocatively as to attract a brother with her body. Our ancient mothers did not dress in this manner, nor did they use this tactic to attract men. Most of the name-brand clothes that the sisters wear today are made by designers who only make their clothes for the European woman. They are made to fit her curves and body structure, but our sisters flock to the malls to buy the designs by Donna Karen, Liz Claiborne, Ralph Lauren, Parasuco, Fendi, etc., because we have not learned to be like ourselves and make our own clothes patterned after our own customs. If sisters dress with their breasts, thighs, and everything out for the world to see, then the chances are that the brothers who are attracted to them will be the brothers who are only out for one thing, and that is SEX!!

SHEIK CHARLES BROWN-EL

Wear your clothes according to the tradition of your foreparents with nothing showing. Then when a brother approaches you, the chances are greater that it will be for all of the right reasons. Sisters, remember that in your dress comes your identity and your self-esteem.

I hear sisters sometimes say that they don't want to cover their heads or wear loose- fitting clothes. I say that in this is immaturity, because the shape or form of your body should not be seen and admired by society. If our sisters will take heed of the voice of Allah and not that of the serpent, as Eve did in the Garden of Eden, then we shall again rise as a people. No nation, regardless of origin, can rise above its women.

The Asiatic woman has been abused and mistreated more than any other woman of any other nationality.

*ACCEPT YOUR OWN AND BE FREE
FROM MENTAL SLAVERY*

During the time of slavery, women suffered much and severely. They were made to fear the slave master, and in turn they instilled the same fear into their children. And so this mentality continues all the way until today, even though today it is more indirect.

The Asiatic man has to be taught how to hold his woman in high regard and understand that she should be highly honored and supported as the queen that she is. She should be taught the knowledge of herself and be able to teach her sisters, so that they can show one another how to be queens and demand to be treated as such. Once our women are raised up in consciousness to know that they have a greater power than being wenches, as the slave master referred to them, then our job is halfway complete, because the woman is the strongest link to any nation. So, brothers, help to uplift fallen humanity. That statement holds a lot of weight, because woman is the symbol of humanity, and Webster's Dictionary defines humanity as "the human race; mankind; people." The woman is the bearer of mankind, and from her womb comes all human life. Brothers, uplift her, support her and love her, and she will honor you. Happy is the man who has made her his wife; happy is the child who calls her mother.

*ACCEPT YOUR OWN AND BE FREE
FROM MENTAL SLAVERY*

CHAPTER 2

MEN NEED A PATTERN FOR THEIR LIVES

ACCEPT YOUR OWN AND BE FREE FROM MENTAL SLAVERY

In today's society the Asiatic brother is trying to find himself. His identity has been lost and as a consequence he has tried to become everyone besides who he is. This mentality has carried over from generation to generation. Every twenty years or so we change our names, from Negro, to Colored, to Black, to Afro-American to African-American. It is far more critical for brothers of the Asiatic nation to learn about themselves and know that they should not be identified by the names that refer to slavery (Negro, Black and Colored, etc.).

Life is a cycle of events reoccurring, so there is nothing new under the sun. Our mental condition dates back to when we were held as slaves. We were called bucks by the slave master, and we had sex with many of the slave women in order to bear more children to tend to the slave masters' growing businesses. Now today it is the happening thing in the street to have sex with as many women as possible and tear our sisters down mentally, so that their self-esteem and self-worth is low and their expectations of a man are low.

During slavery, the slave master referred to his property as "my nigger." And what is the term today on the street amongst our brothers as a sign of affection to another brother? We have got to begin to realize that to be a nation we have to return to thinking as a nation, and think as our forefathers thought and not as Negroes, Blacks, or African Americans.

If you have seen the movie *Roots*, remember the main character Kunta Kinte, and the brother who dated Kunta's daughter Kizzy. Sam Bennett was born in America as a slave and he didn't dream to be anything but a slave, because he thought that was all Asiatics were put on Earth for. Kunta, however, never gave up his birthright; all the way to his grave he proclaimed himself to be a Mandinka Warrior, a Moslem, and a man with principles who was mentally free even though he was physically in bondage. Today we have the same brother as Sam Bennett amongst us in society, who never wants anything for himself; he just wants to work for the European all of his life and retire from his job with a small pension. But when a brother comes along explaining to him that he has to learn to do for himself and that he has a heritage, the Sam Bennett brother is offended. He doesn't want to hear about who his people are or how to get free.

We have been oppressing ourselves long enough (yes, we oppress ourselves) by not attempting to connect with our ancient forefathers' divine and national principles. The European was forced to release us from physical bondage, but now we choose to stay enslaved. A man is defined as one who accepts responsibility and supports his family financially, spiritually, emotionally, etc. We have to learn how to provide for our families in the way that we provided in ancient times.

Before we came to these shores of North America, we ruled as Moors and civilized the whole world. But now we live in an uncivilized society, and we brothers have adapted to every way that is so much outside of us being ourselves. There is only one way for the "Negro problem" to be solved, and it comes only through an connection with the Moorish Science Temple of America. Prophet Noble Drew Ali was ordained to be

ACCEPT YOUR OWN AND BE FREE FROM MENTAL SLAVERY

the father of our nation. He was divinely prepared to teach us the truth about our nationality and birthrights. The Prophet brought us back our Moorish flag (a red flag with a five pointed green star in the center), which flies at the United Nations with flags of other nations. Which flag represents "Negroes"? Once our men stand up, take our place in the affairs of men, and learn how to present ourselves as civilized people, we can then teach our women, who in turn will teach our children, and our nation will begin to sprout into the mighty nation that we once were and rule as we once ruled, as Moors.

Prophet Drew Ali laid the blueprint and a path to follow, the path that he walked ahead of us. All we have to do is walk in his footsteps up the path to salvation. Asiatic men should know that we aren't here to be pimps or abusers of our women, but to be the supporters of our nation. Brothers, stop calling your sisters vulgar names. Stop calling one another "dawg", "Nigga", "playa" and all the derogatory names that the European gave you. Return everything that he gave you back to him, because it's not yours. You have your own way of living. Our forefathers didn't hang on the street corners and sell drugs to one another at all hours of the night. They didn't abuse alcohol, marijuana, Ecstasy, PCP, and all the other harmful substances that we put into our bodies. They didn't purchase pistols to shoot one another down as we do today just to get a name in the streets. Wake up, my dear brothers, and see how in our freedom to choose our own destiny we are killing our nation.

*ACCEPT YOUR OWN AND BE FREE
FROM MENTAL SLAVERY*

It's time we follow the path to righteousness and return the church and Christianity back to the European, because it was prepared by their forefathers for their earthly salvation, while we, the Moorish Americans, are returning to Islam because it was founded by our forefathers for our earthly and divine salvation. The brothers aforementioned are all under Rome's system of the church and Christianity, and these are all of its principles. I'm not speaking radically against any group, but we have to accept our own and be ourselves, just as our ancestors were before 1774. Together we stand; divided we fall!

CHAPTER 3

NATION- BUILDING TIME

ACCEPT YOUR OWN AND BE FREE FROM MENTAL SLAVERY

The honorable Marcus Mosiah Garvey said, "Up you mighty nation of people, you can accomplish what you will." It's time we begin to accomplish some mental freedom and some earthly and divine salvation as a people. The time has come when every nation must worship under its own vine and fig tree, meaning the nationality and religion of its forefathers.

You are today without a doubt or contradiction what your forefathers were, and this government places its trusts upon names and issues formed by its forefathers; so we will never be recognized until we all proclaim our nationality and are recognized by the government.

We have to raise the first and smallest nation, which is our households. Brothers, you must be men and support your family. Sisters, be women and obey your God-fearing husband, take care of your children and look after the duties of your household. Children, obey your father and mother and be industrious. After this perfect foundation that was laid by Allah through his prophets, we can begin to raise a beautiful Moorish nation under the five highest principles known to man, which are love, truth, peace, freedom, and justice. The Asiatic family, if properly molded, is the greatest sight to see, especially today when it is nearly extinct, because the majority of our brothers are incarcerated or in graves. The ones who are on the streets commonly use our sisters as slaves and have no desire to commit to one and be the father of a family. This is not true in all cases, but it is true more often than not.

Because of the present conditions, the percentage of Asiatic families that are separated is extremely high. The sister is left alone to play the role of mother and father, because most of the time the brother is not man enough to accept responsibility, or the sister forces him out with her independent I-don't-need- a-man ego. Either way, most of the time she ends up being a single mother on welfare, Section 8, and all kinds of government assistance, with no man to support her and the children. Such behavior has also been carried over from slavery. When the slave master wanted to sell his human property, he would break up families and leave the woman alone with no father or husband to support her and raise the children up to be strong. In our community, we have young Asiatic brothers growing up with no father or positive role model in their lives, so they are forced to revert to the street for everything they need, with the aim of finding themselves.

SHEIK CHARLES BROWN-EL

In order for us to build a nation, there should be a drastic change in our approach to family. A brother should have strong intentions of marrying the sister who bears his child, so that the two are bound by cords to be one flesh. The sister should mean more to the brother than what she has meant in the past to our brothers ("my baby's mother," as she is oftentimes referred to by the brothers in the street). She is "the" queen of the family nation, and "a" queen in the Moorish nation. Asiatic men and women must work with one another and examine one another closely while dating to be sure that this person is a soul-mate before going too far into a relationship. On your present choice depends your future happiness.

This is the time to start building the nation, beginning within our individual selves and then spreading amongst the entire nation. From olden times it has been proven that the so-called Negro has been made to be less than the European. We were forced to serve other Gods and ideals, when it is clear that our forefathers were Moslems. We were taught to believe that we were nothing in the eyes of God, because we were led to believe that a picture of a man with blonde hair, blue eyes and a pale face was our savior and taught that this was our God. Upon seeing this, an Asiatic's subconscious mind begins to think and ponder on his self-worth and whether his hue has a negative effect on civilization. If you are taught that God is a European, and taught that this European man controls everything earthly, and now find out he controls the spiritual realm also, then you feel inferior and lowly about yourself and your kind. This is and was the beginning of self-hate.

Today we are coming out of this philosophy and we are beginning to realize that Jesus was indeed an Asiatic, and that he was not God as we have been made to believe, but that he was a Prophet of Allah who was sent to bring the everlasting gospel of Allah. However, this is only the beginning. There is so much more of our heritage and identity that we've totally gotten away from. Most of us have no desire to find it because of the condition we've been forced to find ourselves in. Unless you are living on a planet outside of earth and not current to what's going on, then you should know that every nationality is recognized by the government under which we live and by the nations of the earth except the so-called black people. We have

*ACCEPT YOUR OWN AND BE FREE
FROM MENTAL SLAVERY*

no land to call our own, no power as other nations, and definitely no love of self. We should now begin to take a look at ourselves as a nation of people and determine what kind of progress we've made thus far in uplifting the nation.

Come and link yourselves back to the families of nations, because in these days it is definitely nation-building time.

CHAPTER 4

DIVINE AND NATIONAL ENLIGHTENMENT

ACCEPT YOUR OWN AND BE FREE FROM MENTAL SLAVERY

According to the Holy Bible, in Deuteronomy 18:18, and the Holy Qu'ran of Mecca, Surah 10:47 and Surah 16:36, every nation was sent a prophet who spoke the language of the people and looked like the people that he was sent to. Jesus was a prophet who was sent to the lost sheep of the house of Israel (Holy Bible: Matthew 15:24). Jesus was sent to save the Israelites from the iron hand of oppression of the pale-skinned nations of Europe, who were governing a portion of Palestine at that time.

The prophet who was sent to the Asiatics of America was Noble Drew Ali, and this prophet came to warn the nation to repent from their sinful ways of clinging to the names and principles that refer to slavery (Negro, Black and Colored, etc.) and return to their forefathers' divine and national way. We should stop serving carnal customs and the mere ideas of man, because they have never done us any good; they have only harmed us as a nation.

A man gets his nationality from the geographical location that his forefathers inhabited. It is Prophet Noble Drew Ali's will for his people to always claim their descent. Since Italians, Chinese, Japanese, etc. are forced to proclaim their free national name and religion before the constitutional government of the United States of America, it is no more than right that the law be enforced upon all other American citizens alike. When we learn of the true nature of our descent and principles, our condition as a people will change almost overnight. Among the descendants of Africa there is still much wisdom to be learned.

*ACCEPT YOUR OWN AND BE FREE
FROM MENTAL SLAVERY*

The Dred Scott decision of 1856 tells us that the Negro has no rights that a citizen is bound to respect. Judge Roger B. Taney of the Supreme Court made a law that a Negro is three-fifths of a human being, which is still the law today, because it hasn't since been amended or altered in any way. According to the United States Constitution, therefore, three-fifths is considered life, liberty, and the pursuit of happiness. The other two-fifths is nationality and religion, which makes a whole man. This is why the so-called Negro always finds himself in a predicament. Some call it racial profiling when the police randomly stop a person because his skin his dark and he is driving a particular type of car. At that juncture the police proceed to abuse and mistreat the individual for no apparent reason. The person's only "crime" is "driving while black." This happens because a Negro is classed as an undesirable and entitled to all the mistreatments and abuses that the police care to bestow upon them. We are willing to be enslaved because we do not accept and proclaim our nationality amongst the governments under which we live.

All of our issues as Negroes are represented and heard under civil rights, which are granted as privileges and can be taken away at any time. Why do we continue to fight for civil rights? When citizens have divisive issues, they fight for and sue for human and equal rights, which are the rights of citizens.

If you have race pride and love your race, then become a part of the Moorish Science Temple of America, where you can learn who you are and who your forefathers were, and take your place among the affairs of men. There is no man who can change the descendant nature of his forefathers unless his powers extend beyond the universal Creator Allah.

Prophet Noble Drew Ali teaches that the changing of our names was an act of European psychology. Johann F. Blumenbach who was spoken of previously, was a German philosopher who came up with a color caste system where he classified everyone by his or her origins in the world. The black race was inferior to the yellow, red, brown, and white races, he claimed, and the white race was superior to all.

This is part of the trickery that makes us hate one another so much. How do we learn to love instead of hate? The Moorish Science Temple of America is where the salvation of the so-called Negro rests. Find the nearest one and join.

CHAPTER 5

MOORISH FLAG

ACCEPT YOUR OW
FROM M

Every nation in the world is recogni flag represents the people of a particular land, and is the identity and heritage of that nation. If there is a nation, then there has to be a flag that flies in the name of that nation, or else there is a dead cat on the line. The so-called black people in America have no flag that flies in their name to came in honor of their fore-parents. The only flag that represents black people is the red, black, and green banner, which they call the African American flag. In this is foolishness; if every nation in Africa has a flag that represents them, then who are you to make your own flag to represent the whole continent? This banner has not been recognized as a flag, because the non-Asiatics will not give this a false sense of dignity, and we, being in utter darkness, cannot force acceptance upon a civilized world.

The flag that represents the so-called blacks in America is the Moorish flag, but it represents us as Asiatic (race) Moorish American (nationality) Moslems (religion). This flag, as stated previously, was the flag of our ancient forefathers that General George Washington chopped down in symbols, and had it stored at 6th and Chestnut Streets in Philadelphia, Pennsylvania. In the year 1774, Philadelphia was the nation's capital.

Prophet Drew Ali visited President Woodrow Wilson in 1912 and asked for the return of the Moorish flag to the Asiatic nation. President Wilson informed the prophet that he wouldn't know where to find the Moorish flag, but the prophet being divinely prepared, knew that the flag was stored in a room with all of the other conquered nations' flags, and was given

ACCEPT YOUR OWN AND BE FREE FROM MENTAL SLAVERY

permission to retrieve it. Since then the Moorish flag has been flying in front of the United Nations, where it was introduced in 1912.

The Moorish flag has an illustrious history involving the ancient Moabites. The flag is over 10,000 years old, but was not always a red flag with a five-pointed green star in the center; it has been changed over time. At one time the flag was white with green Arabic writing on it that stated, "THERE IS NO GOD BUT ALLAH." In battle the flag turned red, symbolic of the bloodshed.

The present flag has in the center the star of Suleiman, a Turkish Sultan from the 1500s. This flag became the national flag of Morocco in 1956 when the country gained its independence from the rule of the French. However, Prophet Drew Ali and the Moorish Science

Temple of America have flown this flag since 1913 A.D., at the inception of the movement. This is proof that it is the Moorish flag and not the Moroccan flag. Investigation will show that the Prophet had the flag first as the flag of the Moorish nation before Morocco adopted it as its flag. Remember, the present people who occupy the land of Morocco are Moorish, but they amalgamated with the French, so they are strangely mixed. However they are still our family—the Moabites.

It is imperative to understand the importance a flag has to the history and identity of a people. Every people shall pitch by their own standard with the ensign of their father's house (Holy Bible: Numbers 2:2) and be recognized by all American and foreign citizens alike.

*ACCEPT YOUR OWN AND BE FREE
FROM MENTAL SLAVERY*

CHAPTER 6

WHY ARE WE MOORISH AMERICANS?

*ACCEPT YOUR OWN AND BE FREE
FROM MENTAL SLAVERY*

Question #14 of the *Koran Questions for Moorish Americans* asks, "Why are we Moorish Americans?" The answer is, "because we are descendants of Moroccans and born in America." As stated earlier, we are not descended from the present day Moroccans because they have amalgamated with the French; therefore they are not the original Moroccans (ancient Moabites). We Moorish Americans are descendants of the ancient Moabites who inhabited the northwestern and southwestern shores of Africa. During the slave trade, this was the land (northwestern and southwestern shores of Africa) where the slaves that were taken directly from Africa were transported. At that time those shores were considered the old Moroccan empire, and so everyone accepted themselves as Moors who were of African descent and there was no such thing as a Negro. You are today without a doubt or contradiction what your forefathers were.

Prophet Noble Drew Ali was divinely prepared to teach us these truths; it has been too long that this information has been kept back from us. Prophet Drew Ali teaches that because we are a people who constantly separated in the world and adopted the customs of different tribes, then we may not know the specific tribes in Africa that we were descended from, but we do know that all of the tribes were Moors.

The prophet teaches that every nation of people has a free national name that they are recognized by. So if other nations have free national names, then why not we? We have been given names that are not of our ancestry, because the slave master named us after him, but we never were given back our names and principles after slavery (Holy Bible: Leviticus 25:10). Therefore, we kept the slave master's name. For example, my last name given at physical birth was Brown; this name is of English descent. It is the free national name of a man or woman from England, not of a Moor. At baptism or obligation to the Moorish Science Temple of America the name EL was annexed to my last name given at physical birth, and thus I reunited with my forefathers as a Moorish American and I became Brown-EL.

The prophet taught the Moorish Americans that our free national names were "EL" and "BEY." EL means God or spiritual lawgiver, and BEY means governor or spiritual law enforcer. These names are of Moorish descent, so if you know anyone who carries one of those names, know that they have denounced the names Negro, Black, and Colored, etc. and have proclaimed themselves to be an Asiatic Moorish American Moslem. And if you meet a man of European descent and he says that his name is "Paul Trevino," then this man is of Italian descent, and "Trevino" is one of the free national names of an Italian. Likewise with "Hector Rodriguez"; you would know that he is of *Latino* descent and that "Rodriguez" is one of his free national names.

What is your free national name as a Black person? Is it Johnson, Smith, Jackson, Thomas, Nelson, Brown, Hall or any of the other names that we carry that do not belong to us?

Prophet Noble Drew Ali attended the Sixth annual Pan American conference in Cuba in the year 1928. Present at this conference was President Calvin Coolidge, who was the President of the United States at that time. Also present were heads of nations all over the world. The prophet was recognized at that very convention as a head of state, meaning that he was the President of the Moorish nation. He is therefore the father of our people, whether we accept it or not. Mostly the Asiatic of America reject it because we haven't been taught anything about our prophet.

The prophet said in a message to the Moors, "If the European and other nations are helping me, then why not you? It is your problem, and the Negro problem is being solved only as it can be, and it is through the Moorish Divine and National Movement in North America."

SHEIK CHARLES BROWN-EL

The question, "Why are we Moorish Americans? can be expounded on a great deal. It's a question of great significance to the Asiatic nation that clings to the marks Negro, Black, and Colored. Come and link yourselves with the missing link and let us uplift ourselves as a nation. Find a Moorish Science Temple of America in your area and bring your questions. If you can't find a Temple, contact the author for assistance. Each one, teach one; get and give.

*ACCEPT YOUR OWN AND BE FREE
FROM MENTAL SLAVERY*

CHAPTER 7

THE CHILDREN ARE OUR FUTURE

ACCEPT YOUR OWN AND BE FREE FROM MENTAL SLAVERY

Seeds are as perfect as the source from which they come. The child is as perfect as the mother is. In the Asiatic family it is a must that we guide our children's hearts and minds, to raise them in the way that they should go, and when they get older they will not depart from it. We as parents must consider that we have to guide and set our children right in their youth and let no evil habit gain strength with their years, because through the womb of the Asiatic woman come the guiders of our nation. We must teach and instruct our children to stay on the right path, and not just to go to school and become something by graduating and getting a good job with the European; we must teach them about themselves. Teach them about their nationality and religion, and from this they will grow to do the same from generation to generation. In order to teach and instruct the babies, we have to first be instructed and taught as to who we are and why we are here.

Before we begin to plan to have children, we should know and understand already how we are going to rear this child. The master word is **"PLAN."** As a student, my Grand Sheik, which is the title of the head official in the Moorish Science Temple of America, would oftentimes instruct me to plan. He would say that this was the word that I should ponder on. Before bringing a child into this world, brothers and sisters should be mentally and spiritually ready to conceive this child. You should talk to one another about having a child, and then you should begin to change your diet if it isn't already a good one. You should seek revival of your strength and summon the spirit of the almighty God-

ACCEPT YOUR OWN AND BE FREE FROM MENTAL SLAVERY

Allah. During the pregnancy, brothers, speak good words to your sister woman and let the kindness of your behavior be acceptable to her. Whatever she is feeling or thinking, it is directly fed to the unborn baby. So if you're constantly not around, or if you are fighting and arguing, then your unborn child is being exposed to all of this, and you could be jeopardizing the health and well-being mentally and physically of both the child and the mother. Remember to receive your wisdom from the great God-Allah and always plan, because on your present choice depends your future happiness.

Prophet Noble Drew Ali stated that he came for the young and the unborn; the old could come if they wanted. He knew you couldn't put new wine in old skins because it would burst them. The older we get, the more we get set in our ways. The young and unborn, by the guidance of Allah through the parents, will sprout into strong Moorish leaders and make a gigantic step in removing our nation, the Moorish nation, from mental slavery. The son that does right is an honor to his father's gray hair.

*ACCEPT YOUR OWN AND BE FREE
FROM MENTAL SLAVERY*

CHAPTER 8

THOUGHT IS THE CAUSE OF IT ALL

ACCEPT YOUR OWN AND BE FREE FROM MENTAL SLAVERY

Philosophers and doctors of law have taught us ever since the days of old that what we think will manifest itself into physical existence. The law of karma is defined basically as: What we reap, we sow. This also is the law of cause and effect, which is that what goes around comes back around again. The power of our minds is great. Have you ever made yourself feel sick by telling yourself that you were, just so you could take the day off from work, and then you began to really take ill? This was so all because of your thinking.

As a nation, we as Asiatics are a very hateful race of people. We think negative thoughts about our brothers and sisters on a daily basis, when in fact if we would just uplift them we would feel much better about ourselves and pretty much keep negative karma out of our lives. When you have a harmful thought, you do harm to Allah, because every living thing is bound by cords to every other living thing. How could you say that you love God whom you've never seen and hate your brother or sister whom you see every day when man was made in the image and likeness of God? Hate is a cruel word; it is an action. When you talk about and judge others, scorn others, or violate anyone it is hate, and you will pay for it later. Think not, bold man, because your punishment is delayed that the arm of Allah is weakened. You will get back everything that you deserve in due time. If you want to serve Allah, just serve your near kin and those who are not kin, the stranger at your gates, the foe who seeks to do you harm. When someone harms you and is evil toward you, do not return the evil and hate with evil and hate;

just give their injustice a friendly admonition and turn the hate of men into love, and Allah is pleased.

We have been through so much with slavery, racism, etc. that we have turned into a very cruel and selfish nation of people. Once we know that if we change our thoughts we will begin to change, then we will collectively begin to watch the ways in which we think. There is nothing that we do that does not stem from a thought. This is so because Allah gave man a will to choose, so we accomplish only what we set our minds on to accomplish. To animals he gave instinct so they do only what they are intended to do. We as Asiatic Moorish Americans should soon figure out that our sinful thoughts are the reasons why we constantly have confusion and chaos in our lives. Jesus said, "The sin lies in the wish, in the desire, not in the act." Man was put on earth and intended to live the good life. That does not mean that trials and tribulations do not come, but that is exactly what they are, TRIALS AND TRIBULATIONS. God-Allah does not intend for any man to go through chaotic retributions; it is only of man's own will. When you are being tempted know for certain that it is your lower self tempting you, and not Allah (Holy Bible: James 1:12-14).

Man has two selves, the higher self and the lower self. The higher self is the mother of virtues and the harmony of life that breeds justice, mercy, love, and right. The lower self is hatred, slander, lewdness, murder, theft, and everything that harms. If your thoughts are from your higher self then your life will be filled with prosperity. If your thoughts are constantly from your lower self then your life will be filled with disappointments and crisis. Why wouldn't we want our lives to be prosperous, our cups running over with goodness? There are things and activities in our daily lives that need to be corrected for us to really be recognized by all other nations of the world.

Brothers and sisters, try to control your thinking and begin to think good thoughts on a daily basis. I know it is rough, because most of us are in a down- trodden position, but we must take the first step of letting Allah come into our hearts and minds and keeping good clean thoughts. When you do this, see if your earthly and heavenly conditions change, because Allah is love and Jesus, Mohammed, Buddha, Confucius, Noble Drew Ali, and all of Allah's prophets came to manifest that love to men. The man who can control his thinking can rule the world, because his thoughts bring everything into manifestation. As a man thinks, so is he. If you think you are great then you are; if you are ashamed of yourself and have no self-worth then the world will feel the same way toward you.

The thoughts of Allah cannot be circumscribed; they are from the everlasting days of the past unto the never-ending days to come. Man was a thought of Allah that was manifested and brought forth to be the lord of the plane of things made manifest, and man was given control and dominion over everything on earth. He was given the right to name and delegate every living thing. So man is sort of a god, not the great God as some would believe. Man's thought was not of things heavenly, so he debased himself from Allah and fell, and the carnal nature sprang forth. Because of man's thoughts the lower self came into existence, which is considered to be hatred, slander, lewdness, murder, thefts, and everything that harms. Because of the lower self we cannot attain things heavenly; everything that we desire is of the flesh, an illusion, and will pass away at some point.

The fallen sons and daughters of the Asiatic nation need to learn to love instead of hate, and learn of their higher self and lower self. Recognize that all thoughts of Allah are on high. So man, you are the husbandman of everything that ever was, is, or evermore will be. Think like God, be godly, and control your thoughts.

CHAPTER 9

ESTABLISH PRINCIPLES OF ACTION

ACCEPT YOUR OWN AND BE FREE FROM MENTAL SLAVERY

Love, truth, peace, freedom, and justice must be taught universally to all nations, for these are the five highest principles known to man. Through these principles we can learn to pattern our lives. The man who demonstrates love, truth, peace, freedom, and justice as prescribed by Prophet Noble Drew Ali will be well liked by all who know him or come into contact with him. If our nation would learn to exercise these principles, then we would be on the road to salvation and mental freedom.

Principle, as it is defined in the dictionary means "a rule of conduct," and blessings attend the person or persons who conduct themselves under love, truth, peace, freedom, and justice, because it is through these principles that the senseless killings will stop, it is through these principles that youth will stop using drugs, and it is through these principles that the so-called Negro will accept his own and know that he is not Negro, Black, or Colored, but that his nationality is Moorish American, his race is Asiatic, and his religion is Islam. Having principles is a very important part in raising a nation. Every nation under the sun has principles that they forever act according to. As it stands, the Asiatic of America has no principles; anything goes.

We have no land to call our own, we produce no agriculture, and everything we buy we have gotten from someone else. We spend more money than any other nationality of people, and all the money we spend leaves our community and goes into other nations' treasuries. We have to open stores and support our own business ventures collectively as a whole for the good of the nation. We must exercise our talents and skills so that other nationalities can move their businesses from our neighborhoods and stop getting rich off our ignorance and we can move our own businesses in and build our nation's treasury, generate finance in our circle, and gain economic security, which is one of our greatest needs. But first we must adhere to the principles of love, truth, peace, freedom, and justice and be ourselves.

The time has come when every nation shall strive to be like its forefathers; our forefathers, the ancient Moabites, were not a beggar people. They were upright, independent and fearless. In this day and age we have to understand the way that families of nations work. We need agriculture, we need economic security, and first and foremost we need love—love of self and love of Allah. A beggar people cannot attain the highest in them, so if we constantly attempt seeking out employment through the European and every other nation instead of having businesses of our own through which we employ one another, then we can never be truly uplifted. We raise our children with the thought in their minds to be something by growing up and getting a job. Never do we teach them to struggle and work hard at doing for self and operating their own businesses as other nationalities do. Nor do we start a business so that we can teach our children a work ethic and how to control their finances so that they can inherit the business as the European teaches his children.

Other nationalities have principles that they were blessed with and that they follow obediently; they have been blessed to the point that they are very wealthy. Their children grow up and inherit the business and keep it operating smoothly because they are taught how to. Here is a thought: Have you ever come across a business that sort of appears out of nowhere, and the logo reads, **"been in business for 50 years"**? You say to yourself, "How come I have never heard of this company?" That's because most of the time the owner's parents or grandparents incorporated the business name 50 years ago for their offspring, and never did anything with the business, but when the offspring reached adulthood he had an incorporated business that he could open up if he desired, using his talents. When a potential client comes along and checks local state records for this business, they will see the length of time the business has been active and be more inclined to do business with an establishment that has a history.

We must teach our children from the womb how to prepare themselves to do for self, so that we can have our own as a people as all other nationalities do. These five principles: love, truth, peace, freedom, and justice, must be proclaimed and practiced by all who are descendants of Africans and born in America, because these principles are of God and God is the greatest. ALLAHU AKBAR!

*ACCEPT YOUR OWN AND BE FREE
FROM MENTAL SLAVERY*

CHAPTER 10

ISLAMISM!

ACCEPT YOUR OWN AND BE FREE FROM MENTAL SLAVERY

Islam is the study of peace. The very name "Islam" means peace—peace with everything, peace with man, peace with your surroundings. Prophet Noble Drew Ali says that the religion of the so-called Negro in North America is "Islamism," which is the practice of Islam socially, spiritually, economically, financially, judicially, and politically. In the United States of America, the so-called Negro has been conditioned to believe Islam is about terrorism. There is nothing further from the truth. This is a misrepresentation and a trick of the mind to keep you, the Asiatic of America, from linking with your illustrious history. The goal of a man's life in Islam is strictly to obtain peace.

In a previous chapter it was stated that when a man harms another man in thought he does harm to Allah. A Moslem wants for his brother or sister what he wants for himself. He is a noble man who is himself what he believes all men should be. The definition of a Moslem is one who submits his will to Allah. Let's take a close look at that. If you put your will in harmony with the will of Allah, then all is well. Man has his own will to choose, and if your will is of your higher self and it is divine, then it is the will of Allah. The will of Allah is never to hurt anyone in thought, word, or deed, because Allah is love. Prophet Noble Drew Ali teaches us that we need to learn to love instead of to hate, and to know of our higher self and lower self. We the Asiatic in America should be taught how to love, because so much has been passed down to us through the years that all we know is hate, directly and indirectly.

ACCEPT YOUR OWN AND BE FREE FROM MENTAL SLAVERY

There is only one God, and the world sees him from different points of view. All of the nations of the earth call him by different names. The Hebrews call him Jehovah, the Greeks call him Thoth, and the Moslems call him Allah. He is the causeless cause and the rootless root from which all things grow.

In these times, every nation must worship under its own vine and fig tree. As was stated previously, the vine and fig tree are nationality and religion. The nationality of all of those who call themselves Negro, Black, Colored, and African American is Moorish American, and their religion is Islamism whether they accept it or reject it.

Islam and its principles are righteous for the salvation of our people. There are things that are right and then there are things that are righteous. Something can be right to you but not be righteous. Right is when it benefits one, and righteous is when it benefits all. When the European nations bound the Asiatic nation in slavery, it was right to them because they believed that our people were born to be slaves. It also assisted them with their growing businesses, but it wasn't righteous because it tore up our families. We were robbed of our culture and religion and a great many of us were murdered. Islamism is right for our people as well as righteous for our people because once we all are practicing Islam and return Christianity back to the European nations, then the prophecy will be fulfilled that the lion and the lamb can lie down together in yonder hills and neither will be harmed in the morning, according to the Prophet Isaiah in the Holy Bible. The lion is symbolic of the European race and the lamb is

ACCEPT YOUR OWN AND BE FREE FROM MENTAL SLAVERY

symbolic of the Asiatic of America. As long as the European nations were in their church and got our people into the church, then there was no peace. Therefore it is only right for the European and not righteous for all, because Christianity was prepared by his forefathers for his earthly salvation.

Brothers and sisters, learn of your forefathers' way, and begin to practice it and live it that we can grow and dispel all myths about our race and culture. May Allah the God of love guide us all and bind our hearts and minds together as was done in ancient times.

CHAPTER 11

TURBAN AND FEZ

*ACCEPT YOUR OWN AND BE FREE
FROM MENTAL SLAVERY*

All nationalities are recognized by the dress of their ancient mothers and fathers, and more often than not they will have clothing and headdress on that will make you know and identify at once who they are. We, the Moorish Americans, have ancient garbs that we are recognized by and we also have headdress.

The national headdress of the Moorish man is the fez. The fez is a brimless hat with a tassel on the top that hangs down from the top. The tassel flows freely around the fez, representing 360 degrees of knowledge. It is crimson-colored, which represents the blood of our ancient forefathers (see the drawing on the cover). However, there are other colors that one can wear once he has attained the position(s) that allow him to wear the specific color.

SHEIK CHARLES BROWN-EL

The fez is a symbol of consciousness. There are other groups and organizations that wear the fez and do not consider themselves to be Moorish Americans. They put symbols on it and tie the tassel down so that it does not flow freely about the fez. The fez as it is in its purest form is our headdress and should be respected and accepted as such.

The national headdress of the Moorish American woman is the turban. The turban is like a crown of glory circling her head (Holy Koran of the Moorish Science Temple of America: Chapter 21:7). It reminds the sister of her divine duty as a woman, and symbolically means that she is wrapped in her right frame of mind. Prophet Noble Drew Ali instructs the sisters to wear the Moorish button in the turban at the center of the forehead to distinguish the Moorish

American Moslem (Holy Bible: Revelation 9:4) from the rest of the world.

One day after we have gotten over our identity crisis and accept our own identity there will be turbans and Fezzes everywhere you look, because we will be honoring our creed and principles.

CHAPTER 12

THE RISE TO GREATNESS

ACCEPT YOUR OWN AND BE FREE FROM MENTAL SLAVERY

The legend of the phoenix bird rising from its own ashes after it has perished is symbolic of the resurrection and a direct likeness of the Asiatic of America. We have suffered severely and have perished from a lack of knowledge of self (Holy Bible: Proverbs 29:18). By the guidance of Allah, through the last prophet in these days who was divinely prepared in due time to save the Asiatic of America from mental slavery, we will rise again to royalty.

As you contemplate the fall of the Moorish empire, one must keep in mind that we were the builders of civilization. The Moors were the founders of mathematics and science, and we taught the European what we knew. In return he robbed us and enslaved us and up until today he is still using what we taught him against us.

When you read the story of Lazarus (Holy Bible: John 1:44) you see a reflection of the Asiatic of America. Whereas it appears as if we are dead and out of it we are not; we just need to be uplifted to the state of consciousness that our forefathers were found in. Then and only then our people as a whole can leave the valley of the dry bones (Holy Bible: Ezekiel 37) and go into the land that Allah has prepared for us, and we shall be his people and he shall be our God.

We shall make it clear and make it known to the world that we are no longer clinging to the names and principles that refer to slavery, and that we are returning the church and Christianity (its principles) back to the European nation, because it was prepared by their forefathers' for their earthly salvation, and it was and is not the religious creed and principles that we should follow. We have a prophet who came to us to take us back in mind of our forefathers' way of thinking and bring us back our principles of love, truth, peace, freedom, and justice which we will always adhere to.

Come to learn of yourself, your true and divine way, and act as your soul dictates, and your end shall always be right.

Peace, and may Allah bless our undertakings in love, truth, peace, freedom, and justice.

Sheik Charles Brown-EL

Son of Allah

Servant to humanity

SHEIK CHARLES BROWN-EL

MOORISH AMERICAN PRAYER

Allah, the father of the universe, the father of love, truth, peace, freedom, and justice, Allah is my protector, my guide, and my salvation, by night, and by day, through his holy prophet Drew Ali, amen.

REFERENCES

1. *Holy Koran of the Moorish Science Temple of America.*
2. *Koran Questions for Moorish Americans.*
3. *Moorish Literature*, by Prophet Noble Drew Ali.
4. *The Resurrection: Moorish Science Temple of America, Inc. The Truth: Be Yourself and Not Somebody Else*, by Timothy Dingle-EL-Noble Drew Ali in this era of time (Library of Congress catalogue card #78-67828).
5. *Holy Bible.*
6. *Holy Qu'ran.*
7. *Webster's Dictionary.*
8. Dred Scott Supreme Court Decision, 1857.

9. United States Constitution and the Declaration of Independence.

10. *Encyclopedia Americana*, International edition, volume 11.

11. *Golden Age of the Moors,* by Ivan Van Sertima.

12. *Moors in Spain*, by Stanley Lane-Poole.

ACCEPT YOUR OWN AND BE FREE
FROM MENTAL SLAVERY

MOORISH SCIENCE TEMPLE OF

AMERICA, INC.

CONTACT LIST

Herein is a list of Temples that you can get in contact with to find out more information about the truth of your identity. Be aware that some of the addresses and phone numbers may have been changed. If none are close to you, call or write to one and ask for information on a Temple in your area. For Moorish American Moslems, if your Temple's information is not here, please forgive me for overlooking you. It is time we begin to uplift ourselves and gain access to some salvation.

SHEIK CHARLES BROWN-EL

Moorish Science Temple of America Inc.

State of Maryland Temple No.13

1055 N. Milton Avenue

Baltimore, Maryland 21205

(410) 522-6633

Moorish Science Temple of America Inc.

43 Osborne Street

Albany, New York 12202

(518) 436-6539

Moorish Science Temple of America Inc.

613 Liberty Street

Camden, New Jersey 08102

*ACCEPT YOUR OWN AND BE FREE
FROM MENTAL SLAVERY*

Moorish Science Temple of America

2412 N. 25th Street

Philadelphia, Pa. 19132

Moorish Science Temple of America, Inc.

Temple No. 5

1324 ½ Lincoln Avenue

Pittsburgh, Pa. 15206

Moorish Science Temple of America, Inc.

Temple No. 11

655 N. 56th Street

Philadelphia, Pa. 19131

(215) 473-0233

SHEIK CHARLES BROWN-EL

Moorish Science Temple of America, Inc.

Temple No. 11

2022 South Street

Philadelphia, Pa. 19146

(215) 985-1250

Moorish Holy Temple of Science

Temple No. 1

51 South 11th Street

Newark, NJ. 07107

(201) 485-5400

Moorish Science Temple of America, Inc.

Temple No. 10

66 North 7th Street

Newark, NJ. 07107

*ACCEPT YOUR OWN AND BE FREE
FROM MENTAL SLAVERY*

Moorish Science Temple of America, Inc.

3810 South Wabash Avenue

Chicago, IL. 60653

(312) 285-3313

Moorish Science Temple of America Inc.

Temple No. 6

2019 N. 28th Street

Richmond, VA. 23223

(804) 783-8351

Moorish Science Temple Of America Inc.

5519 N. 37th Street

Milwaukee, WI. 53209

SHEIK CHARLES BROWN-EL

ABOUT THE AUTHOR

Sheik Charles Brown-EL was born October 3, 1976 in Baltimore, Maryland. At an early age he adapted to the ways of the street.

In 1994, when he was 17 years old he accepted the teachings of Prophet Noble Drew Ali and the Moorish Science Temple of America while incarcerated and has since made a complete change in his life recognizing that he was being called to assist in the program of Uplifting fallen Humanity.

Presently, he resides in Albany, New York and is one of the active officials in the Temple under the leadership of National Grand Sheik Clarence Prather-EL of Suitland, Maryland. He also has assisted in setting aside Temples in Philadelphia, Pennsylvania and Albany, New York.

CPSIA information can be obtained
at www.ICGtesting.com
Printed in the USA
LVHW327220621
69091LV00003B/204